Super Silly School Jokes

Gene Perret
Joseph Rosenbloom
Meridith Berk
&
Toni Vavrus

Illustrated by Sanford Hoffman

Sterling Publishing Co., Inc.
New York

Library of Congress Cataloging-in-Publication Data
Super silly school jokes / Gene Perret ... [et al.] ; illustrated
by Sanford Hoffman.
    p. cm.
    Includes index.
    Summary: An illustrated collection of riddles and jokes
about school.
    ISBN 0-8069-9738-9
    1. Education—Juvenile humor. 2. Wit and humor,
Juvenile. [1. Jokes. 2. Riddles. 3. Schools—humor.]
    I. Perret, Gene. II. Hoffman, Sanford, ill.

PN6231.S3 S86 2001
818'.602—dc21   2001040084

Published by Sterling Publishing Company, Inc.
387 Park Avenue South, New York, N.Y. 10016
This book has been excerpted from *Super Funny School
Jokes* © 1991 by Gene Perret; *Great Book of School
Jokes* © 1994 by Meridith Berk & Toni Vavrus; and
School's Out! © 1989 by Joseph Rosenbloom
© 2001 by Sterling Publishing Co., Inc.
Distributed in Canada by Sterling Publishing
⁰∕₀ Canadian Manda Group, One Atlantic Avenue, Suite 105
Toronto, Ontario, Canada M6K 3E7
Distributed in Great Britain and Europe by Chris Lloyd
at Orca Book Services, Stanley House, Fleets Lane, Poole BH15
3AJ, England
Distributed in Australia by Capricorn Link (Australia) Pty. Ltd.
P.O. Box 704, Windsor, NSW 2756 Australia

Sterling ISBN 0-8069-9738-9

CONTENTS

1. UP AND OUT

My father has a great way of getting me up in the morning. I sleep with two dogs in my bed and when it's time for me to get up, he throws the cat in.

TERRY: Why are you so grouchy today?
JERRY: I got up on the wrong side of the bed this morning.
TERRY: And that makes you grouchy?
JERRY: Sure it does. My bed is next to the wall.

BORIS: What does it take for your Mom to get you out of bed in the morning?
NORRIS: About 45 minutes.

Where do hyenas go to school?
Ha-ha-Harvard.

What school do cats go to?
Purr-due.

Where do clocks go to school?
Georgia Tech-tock.

Where do convicts go to school?
Penn.

What school did Orville Reddenbacher go to?
Pop-Cornell.

What school did Uncle Ben go to?
Rice.

What school does royalty go to?
Duke or Princeton.

What school do toothbrushes go to?
Colgate.

What school do door-to-door salesmen go to?
The school of hard knocks.

What school do comedians go to?
The school of hard knock-knock jokes.

What school do sleepyheads go to?
A nap-olis.

What school is especially for soldiers with a bad sense of direction?
East Point.

What school is named after a farm animal?
Oxford.

What school do bunny rabbits go to?
Johns Hop-kins.

Who tells people where to get off and gets away with it?
The school bus driver.

KID: Is this my bus?
DRIVER: No, it belongs to the bus company.

KID: Can I take this bus to school?
DRIVER: No, it's too heavy to carry.

Why did the little kid go to school on Saturday?
He wanted to be in a class by himself.

Knock-knock.
  Who's there?
Meyer.
  Meyer who?
Meyer late getting to school!

I'm never on time for anything. I was four hours late catching the 24-hour virus.

TONGUE TWISTERS

Say these three times quickly!

Mary's sleepy sheep slept through school.

A new gnu and a blue ewe.

DEAN: Every morning I dream I'm falling from a 10-story building and just before I hit the ground, I wake up.
GENE: That's terrible. What are you going to do about it?
DEAN: I'm going to move into a 15-story building. I need more sleep.

I had a dream last night that I was eating this giant marshmallow. When I woke up, my pillow was gone.

GOTCHA

YOU: (to your friend) Say and spell M-O-O-D.
FRIEND: Mood—M-O-O-D.
YOU: Say and spell F-O-O-D.
FRIEND: Food—F-O-O-D.
YOU: Say and spell B-R-O-O-D.
FRIEND: Brood—B-R-O-O-D.
YOU: Say and spell H-O-O-D.
FRIEND (will probably say): Hoo-ood.

I have a buddy who is late for everything too. It takes her an hour and a half to watch *60 Minutes*.

I like to sleep. That not only explains why I'm late to school, but also my grades.

TEACHER: Young man, do you know what time we start school here in the morning?
WALTER: No, teacher, I don't. I've never been here for that.

TEACHER: Young man, you've been late for school every day this week.
ALVIN: No, teacher, I was only late for school four days this week. The other day I was absent.

TEACHER: You've been late for school five days this week. Does that make you happy?
MITZI: Sure does—that means it's Friday.

MOTHER: Now these new clothes are expensive. I don't want you coming home from school the first day with a hole in the knee.
TOMMY: Okay, Mom, where would you like the hole?

MOM: Lester, you have your shoes on the wrong feet.
LESTER: No I don't, Mom. These are the only feet I have.

I had one friend who lost his shoes one time because he put them on the wrong feet. Then he couldn't remember whose feet he put them on.

DARREN: I wish I was in your shoes.
KAREN: Why would you want to be in my shoes?
DARREN: Because mine have holes in them.

READING LIST

Taking Care of Your Teeth by Pearl E. White

Entering the School by Doris Open

MUFFY: I'm going to bring my
    pet bird to school.
DUFFY: What kind of bird is it?
MUFFY: A keet.
DUFFY: Don't you mean a
    parakeet?
MUFFY: No. I only have one.

JIMMY: Teacher, I don't have a pencil.
TEACHER: How can you come to school without a
    pencil?
JIMMY: I took the bus.

JOHNNY: Teacher, I don't have a pencil.
TEACHER: I want you to write 100 times "I will
    come to school prepared."
JOHNNY: With what?

Why did the kindergarten student want a new
pencil?
The one she had made too many mistakes.

Why does your pencil have an eraser at both ends?
That's so I don't make the same mistake twice.

2. WHAT DID YOU DO THIS SUMMER?

TEACHER: Everyone, please turn in your compositions about what you did this summer. (*Audrey turns in a blank sheet of paper.*) Audrey, your paper has nothing on it. Didn't you have a vacation?

AUDREY: Yes, Teacher. I had a wonderful vacation. I did nothing all summer.

Why is it so hard to do nothing all summer?
Because you can't stop and rest.

When are you most likely to dream about going on vacation?
When you're asleep.

Where did the wolves stay when they traveled?
At a Howliday Inn.

Where did Lassie vacation?
Collie-fornia.

Where did the cows vacation?
Cow-lorado and Moo-souri.

Where did the ducks vacation?
North and South Duck-ota.

I went to a dude ranch. One cowboy there asked
me if I ever rode a donkey.
   I said no.
   He said, "Well, you better get on to yourself."

CLEM: I know how to tell directions by using the stars.
LEM: I do too. If you're getting closer to them, you're going up.

In summer camp I never changed my clothes once. Towards the end the skunks ran away from me.

I came home from camp with 12 pets that I found in the woods. So far, my mother has only found three of them.

What's the best thing to do to keep from getting lost in the woods?
Stay in your room.

What side of a tree does moss grow on?
The outside.

TEACHER: And what did you learn during the summer, Herman?
HERMAN: I learned that three months is not enough time to straighten up my room.

FATHER: Well, son, I promised we would make this trip and now, after thousands of miles, we are finally here. I'll tell you what—since you packed the car, I'll unpack it.
SON: Uh, Dad—I thought you packed the car...

NIT: Do you summer in the country?
WIT: No, I simmer in the city.

What is the best kind of letter to read on a hot day?
Fan mail.

Why did the skeletons vacation alone?
Because they had no-body to go with.

Where did the zombies go on vacation?
Club Dead.

Where did the mummies go on vacation?
The Dead Sea.

What lives in water and takes you anywhere you want to go?
A taxi crab.

Where did the fish go on vacation?
Finland.

Where do people leave their dogs when they go on vacation?
At the arphanage.

How do dogs travel when they go on vacation?
By mutt-a-cycle.

What do people say after a dog takes off on vacation?
Dog-gone!

What dog cools you off on a hot day?
A pup-sicle.

Where do you take a dog for his shots?
To the dogtor.

What is green, has big eyes and lives all alone in the pond?
Hermit the Frog.

What goes "Dit-dot-dot-croak, dit-dot-dot-croak?
Morse toad.

What do frogs wear on their feet during the summer?
Open toad shoes.

What do you say when you meet a toad?
"Wart's new?"

What do you say to a hitchhiking frog?
"Hop in."

THE FOOD AT CAMP WAS SO BAD...

...I threw my dinner in the river one night and the fish threw it back.

...We used to rub it on our bodies to keep insects off.

...The chef had a black belt in cooking.

...Some of the kids at camp got sick. They ate it.

...Food fights were encouraged. They were not only fun, but it was safer than eating the food.

What flies through the night, wears a black cape, and bites people?
A mosquito in a black cape.

Why do mosquitoes bother people most late at night?
Because mosquitoes like a little bite before they go to sleep.

THE MOSQUITOES ON OUR VACATION WERE SO BIG...

...If you swatted them, they swatted you back.

...They had their own landing strip.

...Insect repellent didn't bother them. They just carried you down to the stream and washed it off.

...They not only bit you, they also knocked you down and stole your wallet.

...They kept me awake all night—they kept pushing me out of bed.

TOM: Did you hear about the boy who went swimming in the river on Sunday? When he wanted to come ashore, he couldn't.
DOM: How come?
TOM: The banks are closed on Sunday.

What do you get if a bunch of thieves dives into the pool?

A crime wave.

How do atomic scientists relax?

They go fission.

ELMER: I'm going on a fishing trip and I need some tackle. Please hurry—I have to catch a bus!

CLERK: Sorry, young man—we don't have fishing tackle that big.

Why did Dr. Jekyll go to the beach?

To tan his hide.

Where can you find a haunted beach?

On the sea ghost.

Where does a dinosaur go for vacation?
To the dino-shore.

What do police use to patrol the seashore?
A squid car.

What is black and white and red and hates to be touched?
A sunburned zebra.

3. THE KIDS IN MY CLASS...

One kid in our class was so silly he had his address tattooed on his forehead. That way, when he got lost, he could mail himself home.

Another kid had "left" and "right" tattooed on his toes so he would know which feet his shoes should go on. Now all he has to do is learn how to read.

One kid in our class is so dense, he can't fill in his name on an application form unless it's a multiple-choice question.

I had a friend who was really kooky. He was late to school every day because he kept trying to put his pants on over his head.

We have one classmate who is not too sharp. His mother once bought him some Silly Putty to play with, and it outsmarted him.

One of my classmates is so smart, he knows the answer to every question the teacher asks. He raises his hand so often in class that his underarms are sunburned.

We have a kid in our class who's so smart, he's got more brains in his little finger than I have in my entire family.

I have a photographic memory. So any time I want to know anything, I drop my brain off at Fotomat and it takes a week to ten days to get it back.
It usually comes back blurry.

One kid in our class dresses terribly. The only things that match on him are his belt size and his IQ.

This kid is a really sloppy dresser. You've heard the expression, "Cleanliness is next to Godliness"? Well, with this kid, it's next to impossible.

This guy is such a sloppy dresser—if you ever see him when his shirttail is not hanging out, it means he's not wearing a shirt.

This kid dresses so sloppily, when he was in a minor accident, they sent him home and took his clothes to the emergency ward.

It's hard to describe the clothing this guy wears, but if you saw it growing in your garden, you'd spray it with weed killer.

This kid wears clothes that are so wrecked, the tailor won't even repair them. He has to take them to a body and fender shop.

One kid in our class wears the best of everything. Even in gym class he has designer sweat.

One guy wears a tie to school every day. Now if they could only get him to wear a shirt.

One of the girls in our class is a very neat dresser. She stayed home sick one day because her skirt was mussed.

This girl is so neat—she gives her clothes away to the needy when they get wrinkled.

This character is such a nut about neatness—her blouse got a food stain on it one day and she took it out and shot it.

I had a friend is always getting into trouble. He was kept after school so much, his parents rented out his room.

One buddy of mine was kept after school so much, the only thing he ever learned was how to lock up when he left.

This kid was kept after school so much—when they finally let him go home, he forgot where he lived.

This character was kept after school so much—when his family moved to a new town, it took him three months to find out.

This guy was kept after school so much—the only time he saw the outside world was during fire drills.

TEACHER: Sometimes I think you come to school just to cause trouble.
LEROY: No, but I figure as long as I'm here...

I know one kid who had to bring her parents to school so often, they had a better attendance record than she had.

I know a kid who's always in trouble at school. He may not graduate—he may just be paroled.

Knock-knock.
  Who's there?
Arena.
  Arena who?
You arena lot of trouble!

What vegetables get in the most trouble?
  Cucumbers. They're always in a pickle.

TEACHER: Phoebe, every time I turn around I catch you doing something you're not supposed to be doing. What can we do about that?
PHOEBE: Tell me when you're going to turn around.

One kid in our class is so dense, he took his dog to obedience school. The dog passed; he flunked.

One of my classmates doesn't carry a pocket comb. He says none of his pockets need combing.

We have one really silly classmate. The football coach told him to jog three miles every day. The last time we heard from him, he was somewhere around Wichita, Kansas.

4. WHERE FLIES GO TO LOSE WEIGHT

The food is so bad in the school cafeteria that flies go there to lose weight.

We had mashed potatoes and gravy in the school cafeteria today, and no one could tell them apart.

The food in the school cafeteria is so bad, they sell gravy by the slice.

The only good thing about the gravy in our school lunchroom is that it hides the rest of the food.

I asked for gravy in the school cafeteria today and they said, "One lump or two?"

The gravy they serve at school is so thick, when they try to stir it, the cafeteria spins around.

The gravy in our school is so thick, you have to get a friend to help you soak your bread in it.

The roast beef we had in the cafeteria today was harder than the test we had in history yesterday.

The meat was so tough at lunch today, half the class was kept after school so we could finish chewing it.

I've had tough slices of meat before, but this one stood up and challenged me to a fight after school.

The roast beef they serve in the school cafeteria is so thin and tough, none of the kids eat it. We use it for knee patches.

The food in our school lunchroom is so bad the teachers hand out second helpings as punishment.

Every Friday in the school cafeteria, they serve leftovers—from World War II.

Let me try to describe what the food tastes like in our school cafeteria. Have you ever eaten any of your old clothes?

NELLIE: How do they keep flies out of the kitchen in the school cafeteria?

KELLY: They let them taste the food.

DOLLY: There's a fly in this ice cream.

SCHOOL CHEF: Serves him right, let him freeze.

MOLLY: There's a moth in my soup!

SCHOOL CHEF: That's right. The fly is on vacation.

WALLY: There's a fly in my butter.

SCHOOL CHEF: No, there isn't.

WALLY: Look for yourself!

SCHOOL CHEF: First of all, it's not a fly, it's a moth. Second, it isn't butter, it's margarine.

The food in our lunchroom is so bad, most of the kids say grace before, during, and after the meal.

NED: Did you see the stew they served in the cafeteria today?

TED: No, but I'll see it when they serve it again next week.

They served chicken noodle soup in the school cafeteria today. A kid from third grade got the noodle.

TEACHER: What was the Tuesday Special in the cafeteria?

RAMONA: Meat loaf.

TEACHER: How did it taste?

RAMONA: Like it should have been the Monday Special.

How do they count muffins in the school kitchen? *They have a roll call.*

SIGN IN THE SCHOOL CAFETERIA:

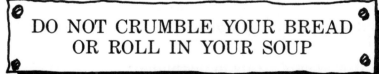

DO NOT CRUMBLE YOUR BREAD OR ROLL IN YOUR SOUP

If we ever study ancient history, the cafeteria will have the rolls to go with it.

This chicken is so old, it knew Colonel Sanders when he was a private.

VERNON: The crust on that apple pie was tough.
SCHOOL CHEF: That wasn't the crust. That was the paper plate.

They threw out leftovers from the school cafeteria yesterday. The alley cats in the neighborhood threw it back.

We had a food fight in the school cafeteria today. The food won.

Our school cafeteria discourages food fights. The food they serve there is dangerous enough without throwing it....Someone might accidentally swallow the food.

What is the worst thing you're likely to find in the school cafeteria?

The food.

The food in the school cafeteria is so bad, last night they caught a mouse trying to phone out for a pizza.

ROB: They served Tuna Surprise in the school lunchroom today.

BOB: I thought that was just tuna sandwiches.

ROB: They were. The surprise comes about an hour after you eat them.

SCHOOL CHEF: Was the chili too hot?
LONNIE: Why, no, smoke always comes out of my
ears.

POLLY: Why is this bread full of holes?
SCHOOL CHEF: It's whole wheat bread.

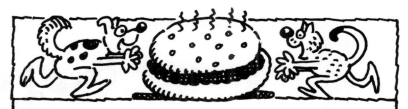

HOW DO THEY LIKE THEIR BURGERS?

How do computer scientists like their burgers?
With chips.

How do musicians like their burgers?
With piccolos.

How do spiders like their burgers?
With French flies.

How do cats like their burgers?
With mouse-tard.

How do sea serpents like their burgers?
With ships.

How do photographers like their burgers?
With cheese.

How do dogs like their burgers?
With Mutts-arella.

What did the baker say to the bread?
"I knead you."

SCHOOL NUTRITIONIST: Eat your vegetables. Green
things are good for you.
WARREN: Okay, I'll have some pistachio ice cream.

Where do you put a very smart hot dog?
On the honor roll.

How did the hot dog wear its hair?
In a bun.

Where do calves eat?
In the calf-eteria.

NEW KID: Is the food in this school any good?
HANS: Sure, if you happen to be a termite.

How do tiny insects cool their lemonade?
With lice cubes.

One of the cooks at our school tried to write a
cookbook, but it came out of the computer burnt.

Knock-knock.
Who's there?
Polynesia.
Polynesia who?
Polynesia cracker.

5. MAKING THE GRADE

My teacher gave me an F-minus. She says I not only didn't learn anything this year, but I probably forgot most of the stuff I learned last year.

TEACHER: Because of your absences, you've missed three tests this week.
RUTHIE: No, I may not have taken the tests, but I didn't miss them one bit.

My teacher says I might as well stay home from school. It's the first thing we've agreed on all year.

My grades are so low, I have to get down on my knees to read my report card.

DIRK: In a class of 21 students, I finished 23rd.
BURKE: That's impossible.
DIRK: No, it's not. Two of the desks got better grades than I got.

DAD: I'm shocked by your report card. You flunked every subject!
JUNIOR: Well, I may not be smart, but I'm really consistent.

My teacher gave me an "f." She said I didn't deserve a capital letter.

I got straight Fs in the sixth grade. That's not good, but it's an improvement over what I did in sixth grade last year.

My dad thinks an F on a report card means "Throw a Fit."

My parents were so ashamed of my grades that on parent-teacher night, they came in disguise.

DONALD: Dad, that teacher flunked me because he doesn't like me. I can read him like an open book.

FATHER: Judging from these grades, I don't think you know what an open book looks like.

FATHER: Judging from this report card, I think you'd better stay in your room every night doing homework.

NICK: Why? Judging from this report card, it's obviously not getting me anywhere.

SONIA: Dad, do you think I can still get into college?
FATHER: With these grades, you'll be lucky to get
  back into school Monday.

My fifth-grade teacher said that she and I have
something in common—we'll both be back in the
fifth grade next year.

This one teacher is so tough with grades, I brought
my parents to school to talk to her about it. She
flunked them.

TESS: Teacher, I wasn't feeling well the day I took
  this test.
TEACHER: I can believe that. Some of the answers
  you gave made me a little sick too.

SON (*showing his report card*): Remember, Dad, Thomas Edison got bad grades in school too.

DAD: Fine, stay in your room until you invent the light bulb.

TEACHER: How long did Thomas Edison live?

SYLVIA: All his life.

My Dad hit the ceiling when I showed him my last report card. If I could only get my grades to go as high as he does!

I was excited when I got my first A in school yesterday. Then I found out it meant Absent.

The only way I can ever get an A is to go on *Wheel of Fortune* and buy one.

FRED: Teacher, I'm a good student, and I deserve better than a D.

TEACHER: What grade would you like?

FRED: Let's see—what's that letter that comes after A again?

ADAM: Teacher, you gave me a zero on this exam. Don't I even get anything for showing up?

TEACHER: What do you think brought you up to a zero?

6. VOWEL LANGUAGE

Knock-knock.
  Who's there?
Eye whites.
  Eye whites who?
Eye whites you a letter in English class.

TEACHER: Can you tell me one word that contains
  all six vowels?
RUDOLPH: Unquestionably.

Why did the a, e, i, o, and u get in trouble?
  They used vowel language.

What's the world's longest punctuation mark?
The 50-yard dash.

Why didn't the English student want to write poetry?
She heard that rhyme didn't pay.

What happened when the English class started writing poetry?
Things went from bad to verse.

What did the little kid use to write his essay about the beach?
Sandpaper.

What did the messy student write with?
A pig pen.

What did the little stream have to do for English class?
A brook report.

TONGUE TWISTERS

Say these three times quickly!

Brenda Brand bought books.

Willie wrote really well.

Please print plainly.

LETTERS LETTERS LETTERS

What letter of the alphabet can fly?
Jay.

What are the three least friendly letters?
NME.

What letter is small and green?
P.

What letter does a sailor love?
C.

What letter is most in debt?
O.

What letters are the smartest?
Ys.

What two letters are the most jealous?
NV.

What are the two coldest letters?
IC.

TEACHER: I'll be teaching you English this year, and there are two words that I will not permit on any of your writing assignments. One is "cool" and the other is "lousy."

WILLIE: Okay, what are the words?

LETTERS LETTERS LETTERS

What letters have nothing in them?
  MT.

What are the two youngest letters?
  BB.

What two letters smell terrible?
  PU.

What two letters are surrounded by water?
  IL.

What are the busiest letters?
  NRG.

What three letters are a musical instrument?
  PNO.

What two letters did Native Americans use?
  TP.

What two letters did you write in English class?
  SA.

TEACHER: Use the word "hyphenated" in a
  sentence.
EVA: There used to be a space between these two
  words, but there isn't any more because the
  hyphen ate it.

TEACHER: Why should we never use the word "ain't"?

ROD: Because it ain't correct.

JOE: I know English good.

FLO: I know English well.

JOE: Good, then both of us ain't gonna flunk the exam.

TEACHER: Mark, please stand and use the word "deceit" in a sentence.

MARK: I would rather sit down because "deceit" of my pants has a hole in it.

TEACHER: What do two negatives make?

PAUL: A double exposure.

TEACHER: What was the pen name of Samuel Clemens?

LOLA: Was it Bic?

7. BY THE NUMBERS...

DAD: As I always say, what you don't know won't hurt you.

SAMMIE: It sure hurt me in the math test I took last week.

TEACHER: What number comes after 4?

VIC: All the rest of them.

What do you call an arithmetic teacher who can make numbers disappear?

A mathemagician.

How far open were the windows in the math class?
Just a fraction.

If you eat two-thirds of a pie, what do you have left?
An angry mother.

If a train is traveling in one direction at 50 miles per hour and another train is coming towards it at 25 miles per hour, when will they meet?
Sooner than they want to.

TEACHER: If you have five people and only four apples, how would you divide them?
PETER: I'd ask someone to get a knife, and whoever was stupid enough to go wouldn't get an apple.

Why couldn't the kindergarten student get any attention?
He didn't count.

How did the math teacher paint a picture?
By the numbers.

What did the math classroom have instead of desks?
Times tables.

What did the math teacher order for dinner?
Cubed steak.

What did the math teacher order for dessert?
Pi.

TEACHER: Remember, class, you can't add apples and oranges.

RORY: My mother does it all the time. She calls it fruit cocktail.

Why did the multiplication table get in trouble with the girls?

He was a two-timer.

How did the little kids like learning addition?

They thought it was a real plus.

What do you call 144 cockroaches?

Gross.

Why was the math student so bad at decimals?

She couldn't get the point.

Teacher: Let X equal the unknown quantity. Now, if X + 10 = 20, and X minus 5 = 5, what is X?

Carl: As far as I'm concerned, it's still the unknown quantity.

Teacher: Can you count from 1 to 20?

Marjorie: I'm not sure. How about if I just count from 1 to 10 twice?

Teacher: Today we're studying percentages. If there are ten questions on a quiz and you get ten correct, what do you get?

Daphne: Accused of cheating.

Why couldn't the 7 and the 10 get married?
They were under 18.

What monster is best at math?
Count Dracula.

MATH READING LIST

Negative Numbers by Morris Les

Basic Math by Adam Upp

Collecting Money by Bill M.

Arithmetic Tests by Kenny Ad

Making the Most of Your Allowance by E.Z. Munny

What would you get if you crossed a dog and a calculator?

A friend you can count on.

How did the student get the answer to 10 minus 10?
He zeroed in on it.

> Knock-knock.
>> Who's there?
> Tennis.
>> Tennis who?
> Tennis half of twenty.

TEACHER: If you had 36 cents in one pocket and 59 cents in the other pocket, what would you have?
GARY: Someone else's pants.

TEACHER: How do you find the square root of 144?
CARLA: I usually ask someone who's smarter than I am.

8. WHAT'S GNU IN SCIENCE?

Why did the bird lay eggs?
Because if it dropped them, they'd break.

Why wouldn't the oyster give up her pearl?
She was shellfish.

How funny was the snake?
Hiss-sterical.

Why couldn't the duck get his medical degree?
He was a quack.

How do you tell how often a tree has been married?
Count its rings.

What tree has the warmest coat?
The fir tree.

How does an alligator use the telephone?
He croco-dials.

Knock-knock.
  Who's there?
Frieda.
  Frieda who?
Frieda bird from da cage.

What do you call a clumsy lion?
King of the bungle.

What insect tells time?
The clock-roach.

TONGUE TWISTERS

Say these three times quickly!

Fleas feel furry.

Green plants, blue pants, red plants.

Luke likes lemmings.

Seeds and seedlings scared Sally.

Peter planted plums.

TEACHER: Who is Isaac Newton?
CLAUDE: I have no idea, but I've heard of his brother, Fig.

What part of a clock is never new?
The second-hand.

THEY NEVER DIE!

Old astronauts never die,
they just space out.

Old photographers never die,
they just get negative.

Old firemen never die,
they just get burned out.

Old radio announcers never die,
they just sign off.

Old planters never die,
they just go to seed.

Old dentists never die,
they just get drilled out of the corps.

Old lions never die,
they just bite off more than they can chew.

Old cartoonists never die,
they just draw a blank.

Old Egyptians never die,
they just sphinx they do.

Old bankers never die,
they just lose interest.

THEY NEVER DIE!

Old movie producers never die,
    they just fade out.

Old bookkeepers never die,
    they just lose their balance.

Old clockmakers never die,
    they just run out of time.

Old boat builders never die,
    they just go under.

Old telephone operators never die,
    they just get disconnected.

Old cleaners never die,
    they just get all washed up.

Old Kentucky Fried Chicken eaters never die,
    they just kick the bucket.

Old crossword puzzle fans never die,
    they just go 6 Down.

Old musicians never die,
    they just tune out.

Old computers never die,
    they just lose their memory.

TEACHER: What does the term "extinct" mean?
CLAIRE: A dead skunk.

TEACHER: What happened to the skunk who backed into the electric fan?
TED: He got cut off without a scent.

How do you groom a rabbit?
With a hare brush.

What are the sneakiest plants?
Creeping vines.

Why did the cat hang around the computer?
She was trying to catch the mouse.

Why don't nature lovers play badminton?
They don't want to hit the birdie.

TEACHER: Tell me which law of physics stops your car.

NINA: When my father is driving, it's usually a policeman who stops our car.

MILTON: I didn't know anything about science before I started going to school.

MOM: Of course not.

MILTON: I still don't know anything, but now they test me on it.

TEACHER: Tell me why the law of gravity is useful.

GLEN: If we drop something, it's much easier to get it off the floor than off the ceiling.

TEACHER: What kind of animal is the bat?

DAVID: It's a mouse that went to pilot training school.

TEACHER: What is H_2O?

RALPH: Water.

TEACHER: What is H_2O_4?

RALPH: To drink.

I cannot walk,
I wear no shoe,
But all the same,
I follow you.
What am I?
Your shadow.

TEACHER: What is a chemical formula?
GRETA: What married chemists feed to their new
babies.

FATHER: Did you finish your chemistry experiment?
SON: Yes—with a bang.

TEACHER: What was that loud noise I heard?
LEE: I think that was the chemistry class flunking
their exam.

MOM: How did you do in your chemistry
experiment?
SON: I don't know. The teacher hasn't come down yet.

TEACHER: How many planets are in the sky?
CANDICE: All of them.

What goes "peckety-peck" and points North?
A magnetic chicken.

What has fur on the outside and feathers on the inside?
A chicken in a mink coat.

TEACHER: What is the outside of a tree called?
SAM: I don't know.
TEACHER: Bark, Sam, bark.
SAM: Bow wow!

What is the most disgusting plant?
Yucca.

In what reference book can you find out about chickens?
In a hen-cyclopedia.

In what reference book can you find out about ducks?
In a duck-tionary.

What would you get if you crossed a small bear and a skunk?
Winnie the Pooh.

What would you get if you crossed a small bear and a cow?
Winnie the Moo.

What would you get if you crossed a skunk and a boomerang?

A smell you can't get rid of.

What part of your body has the best sense of humor?

Your funny bone.

What part of your body is the noisiest?

Your ear drum.

What's the noisiest part of your hand?

Your ring finger.

What part of your mouth has the best vision?

Your eye teeth.

What can you hold but never touch?

Your temper.

What did the weatherman get when he stepped outside into the storm?

A cold front.

Why did the weatherman bring a bar of soap to work?

He was predicting showers.

What would you call it if the sun never set from January to December?

A light year.

What happened when the beam of light broke the law?

It went to prism.

In what kind of home do the buffalo roam?
A dirty one.

Why do birds fly south?
Because if they walked it would be winter by the time they got there.

TEACHER: Why did you fall off your chair?
CLASS CLOWN: I was just demonstrating the law of gravity.

TEACHER: What's a gnu?
CLASS CLOWN: Nothing much. What's a gnu with you?

What game do astronauts play?
Moon-opoly.

Knock-knock.
  Who's there?
Amoeba.
  Amoeba who?
Amoeba rest.

What microscopic animal solves mysteries?
Perry Mecium.

What would you get if you crossed vegetables with
a necklace?
A food chain.

Why was the month so worried?
Its days were numbered.

Knock-knock.
  Who's there?
Dinosaur.
  Dinosaur who?
Dinosaur you at the mall.

What dinosaur worked closely
with the Lone Ranger?
Tontosaurus.

9. OLD TIMES AND NEW PLACES

MUFF: We had a test on the Revolutionary War that was so hard that George Washington would have flunked it.

FLUFF: We had a test last week that was so hard even the teacher flunked it.

TEACHER: When did George Washington die?

REX: Just a few days before they buried him.

What chicken was a famous American patriot?
Pat-chick Henry.

DAD: I don't understand your poor history grades. I always did well in history when I was a kid.
DEXTER: Dad, there's a lot more history now than when you were a kid.

Why did the student miss history class?
He had the wrong date.

Was Rome built in a day?
No, it was built in Italy.

What did they call Caesar when he fell into a vat of dye?
Orange Julius.

What famous French general stepped on a land mine?
Napoleon Blonaparte.

TEACHER: When did Napoleon die?
TAD: I didn't even know he was sick.

Why do kings draw such straight lines?
They are rulers.

Why did the Pilgrims cross the Atlantic on the Mayflower?
It was too far to swim.

Why did the turkey cross the road?
To get away from the Pilgrims.

TEACHER: What does your textbook tell you about the Civil War?

OLIVIA: It doesn't tell me anything. I have to read the dumb thing.

Did you know that Lincoln's assassin had a table in a diner named after him? They call it the John Wilkes Booth.

TEACHER: Name three animals that give milk.

LISA: The goat, the cow, and Mr. Miller who runs the dairy counter at the grocery store.

TEACHER: Did you know that water covers two-thirds of our planet?

ANDY: Certainly. That's why the ocean is always less crowded than the beach.

TEACHER: Go to the world globe and show me where you live.

RITA: I can't. This globe doesn't have a basement.

TEACHER: Where do we find elephants?

CLARK: You can find them anywhere. They're very hard to hide.

TEACHER: Name two cities in Kentucky.

STUART: Okay, I'll name one Dave and the other Irving.

TEACHER: What's the difference between Indian elephants and African elephants?

LENORE: Their zip codes.

TEACHER: On which side of the globe is Central America?
JEFF: On the outside.

EDDIE: I got a 60 on my Map Skills test.
MOM: That's terrible.
EDDIE: I didn't think it was so bad for a kid who wasn't allowed to cross the street until just a couple of years ago.

TEACHER: Where do we find the Suez Canal?
BARRY: It should be written right here on my sleeve along with the rest of the answers.

Who is the coldest relative on earth?
Aunt Arctica.

Where do small dogs like to live?
Lapland.

Are you going to visit Egypt?
I sphinx so.

What is the most precise body of water?
The Specific Ocean.

What do the natives of Peru write with?
Inca.

What is the shakiest national park?
Jellostone.

What would you get if you crossed a river and a desert?
Wet and thirsty.

Why is it so hard to get into the Everglades?
They're always swamped.

What did one person from Holland say to another?
"Let's go Dutch."

What did the explorer say when he found a 5,280-foot rock?
"Now this is a milestone!"

Knock-knock.
  Who's there?
Kenya.
  Kenya who?
Kenya stop asking stupid questions?

Knock-knock.
  Who's there?
Jamaica.
  Jamaica who?
Jamaica my lunch?

Knock-knock.
  Who's there?
Venice.
  Venice who?
Venice Recess?

Knock-knock.
  Who's there?
Yukon.
  Yukon who?
Yukon count to 10.

Knock-knock.
  Who's there?
Juno.
  Juno who?
Juno how old you are?

"Juneau what time it is?"
"Nome, I don't."
"Alaska someone else."

"Boise strange!"
"Idaho—I've seen stranger!"

"Aloha there!"
"Hawaii doing?"

What did Tennessee?
The same thing Arkansas.

What is the most colorful state?
Colorado.

What state has only one actor in it?
The Lone Star State.

What kind of geese come from Portugal?
Portu-geese.

Which country has the most horses?
Horse-tralia.

TEACHER: Where is Greenland?
CHLOE: I don't know.
TEACHER: Where is Bulgaria?
CHLOE: I don't know.
TEACHER: Look them up in your textbook.
CHLOE: I don't know where that is, either.

10. SPELLING AND OTHER TESTS

TEACHER: Can you spell atrociously!
SAMMIE: Sure, and I have the F to prove it.

Our teacher said. "Write your name and today's date on the top of your exam paper. Do it carefully. For many of you it will be the only thing you spell right on the entire page.

TEACHER: Spell "weather."
SETH: Weather. W-A-E-F-H-A-R. Weather.
TEACHER: That's the worst spell of weather we've had in a long time.

TEACHER: Errol, for your homework, I asked you to spell "tomorrow" and you spelled "today."
ERROL: That's because I did my homework yesterday.

TEACHER: Can you spell "banana"?
DIANA: Banana. B-A-N-A-N-A-N-A-N—I can spell it, all right, I just don't know where to stop.

TEACHER: Can you spell "caterpillar"?
MARILYN: How long do I have?
TEACHER: Why?
MARILYN: I want to wait until it changes into a butterfly. I can spell that.

GLORIA: Teacher, how did I do on yesterday's spelling test?
TEACHER: Let's put it this way. Do you know how to spell F?

JIMMIE: Our teacher is giving us another test tomorrow.
MOM: Your teacher is just trying to find out how much you know.
JIMMIE: Then why are all the questions about things we don't know?

If teachers are so smart, how come their book is the only one with the answers in it?

To me, taking a test is like going to the dentist, except after the test you don't get a chance to spit.

HALLIE: Teachers act like they know all the answers.
SALLY: Why shouldn't they? They're the ones that make up all the questions.

Our teacher gives us a test every Friday. The only good thing about it is that it's followed by Saturday and Sunday.

TEACHER: I've given you a multiple-choice exam. What more do you want?
HECTOR: More choices.

NAN: I bite my fingernails before easy exams.
DAN: What do you do when you're taking a hard exam?
NAN: Then I bite other people's fingernails.

PATTY: I get so nervous before an exam that I even forget my own name.
TEACHER: Well, whoever's name you put on this test is flunking the course.

MARVIN: Our teacher told us we should do something to help us relax right before taking an exam.
GARVIN: What are you going to do?
MARVIN: I was thinking about a two-week vacation.

11. HOW MANY BOOKS HAVE YOU READ?

What has a spine but no bones?
A book.

What do librarians hang over their babies' cribs?
Bookmobiles.

LIBRARIAN: Why don't you take home a Dr. Seuss?
MAURICE: I didn't know he made house calls.

My teacher says that we should treat our schoolbooks just like we treat one another. So after school, I picked a fight with my history book.

What would happen if you crossed a locomotive with the author of Tom Sawyer?
A Choo-choo twain.

How did the author of *Tom Sawyer* learn to ride a bicycle?
With twain-ing wheels.

Did you read the dachshund's autobiography?
It's a long story.

What happened when the bloodhound wrote his autobiography?
It got on the best smeller list.

TEACHER: What did you learn from your history book about Harriet Beecher Stowe?
KAREN: If you draw a beard and a stovepipe hat on her, she looks exactly like Abraham Lincoln.

TEACHER: Alex, why are you holding your textbook up to the window?
ALEX: You told us to open it up to the Middle East.

If you don't know what the word "dictionary" means, where would you look it up?

My father gave me a really cheap dictionary for my birthday. I couldn't find the words to thank him.

JASPER: How many books have you read in your lifetime?
CASPER: I don't know. I'm not dead yet.

TEACHER: Gracie, how many books did you finish over the summer?
GRACIE: None. My brother stole my box of crayons.

TEACHER: Connie, tell the class what book you read and then tell them something about the plot.
CONNIE: I read *The Life of Thomas Jefferson*. He dies at the end.

My teacher says our schoolbooks are a magic carpet that will take us all over the world. I took mine to the garage and had them fitted with seat belts.

LIBRARIAN: Did you enjoy reading *Moby Dick*?
ANITA: I couldn't finish it. I got seasick.

SEYMOUR: Do you have *Moby Dick*?
LIBRARIAN: Yes, we do.
SEYMOUR: I thought something smelled fishy in here.

TEACHER: Frannie, tell the class what book you read
    and what you thought of it.
FRANNIE: I read the phone book, but I didn't
    understand it. It had too many characters and not
    enough plot.

LIBRARIAN: Did you enjoy reading *The Hunchback of
    Notre Dame*?
JOSHUA: Well, I read the first 100 pages; then I
    found out it wasn't about football.

TEACHER: Tell the class what book you read.
HARRIET: *Black Beauty.*
TEACHER: And tell the class what it was about.
HARRIET: It was about 120 pages.

Our school library is so quiet you can hear a pin drop—and if it does, the pin is sent to the principal's office.

Our school library is so quiet, when I'm sitting in there, I can hear my hair grow.

Our school librarian is very strict. She'll send you to the principal's office for thinking too loudly.

Why was the little harp sent to the principal's office?
   It was a lyre.

All my schoolbooks have pictures in them—even if I have to draw them myself.

One of my teachers said that I should hand in my books at the end of the year better than when I got them. What does he want me to do—add pages?

My teacher told us that books are man's best friend, so my dog bit him.

12. THE DOG ATE MY HOMEWORK

Well, I figured out what I'm going to be doing in my old age—my homework.

I'm so far behind in my homework that my second grade teacher asked me to bring my parents to school. And I'm in the fifth grade.

TEACHER: Your homework assignment last night was to draw a map of Texas including all the rivers in that state. Why didn't you finish it?

FRANK: I ran out of paper. I thought you wanted it actual size.

MIKEY: Teacher, is there life after death?
TEACHER: Why do you ask?
MIKEY: I may need the extra time to finish all the homework you gave us.

I'm going to lead a long life. That's the only way I'll ever get caught up on my homework.

BETTY: Teacher, this is an awful lot of math homework.
TEACHER: You should be able to complete it if you work hard.
BETTY: Could you throw in one more really hard problem?
TEACHER: Why?
BETTY: It will give my dad something to do so I can get the rest done faster.

TEACHER: This is the first homework assignment you've handed in all week. Why is that?
RICHARD: I was in a hurry last night and didn't have time to think up a good excuse.

I have so much homework...
...it doesn't leave me any time for my studies.
...I may have to drop out of school to finish it.

TEACHER: Geoffrey, what's the definition of "infinity?"
GEOFFREY: Tonight's homework assignment.

TEACHER: Young man, where's your homework?
BOBBIE: It blew away while I was coming to school.
TEACHER: I see. And why are you late to school?
BOBBIE: I had to wait for a strong wind.

TEACHER: That should be enough homework to
keep you busy.
WANDA: That should be enough homework to keep
the Chinese Army busy.

TEACHER: On Monday you said your homework
blew away. On Tuesday you said your father
accidentally took it to work with him. On Wed-
nesday you said your little sister tore it up. On
Thursday you said someone stole it. Today I
asked you to bring your parents to school. Now
where are they?
WILLIE: My dog ate them.

TEACHER: So, your dog ate your homework?

ALICE: Yes, teacher.

TEACHER: And where is your dog right now?

ALICE: He's at the vet. He doesn't like math any more than I do.

It takes me about two hours every night to do my homework—three if my dad helps me.

TEACHER: Anyone who doesn't bring all of the homework to class tomorrow morning will get an F.

TIMMIE: And anyone who does bring all of the homework to class tomorrow morning will get a hernia.

CHARLIE: One kid in our class always said his dog ate his homework.

DAD: That's the oldest excuse in the world.

CHARLIE: Maybe not. His dog graduated from Harvard last week.

SON: Dad, if an airplane leaves Chicago and flies 500 miles an hour west with a 300-mile-an-hour tail wind coming East for two hours, and then flies 600 miles an hour with a 100 mile-an-hour tail wind, and then flies 700 miles an hour for two hours with no tail wind, how far will that plane have flown?

DAD: Son, I'll call my office in the morning and have you switched to an easier flight.

13. TIME OUT!

Our teacher said we could do anything we wanted during recess, so I moved to Pittsburgh.

Just my luck. Recess is the only thing in school I'm good at, and they don't give grades in it.

I like recess so much, when I go to college, I may major in it.

Recess is what I've decided to do with the rest of my life.

TEACHER: How can I get you to devote as much energy to your work as you devote to recess?
JASON: Start playing dodge ball in class.

The teacher came to me one day during recess and said, "You're doing nothing but wasting your time."

I said, "I'm sorry. Whose time should I be wasting?"

TEACHER: What's your favorite class in school?
PEGGY: Morning recess.
TEACHER: What's your favorite class after that?
PEGGY: Tomorrow morning's recess.

Why did the basketball player bring a glass of water to gym class?
So he could learn to dribble.

Why was the kangaroo invited to join the basketball team?
He was good at jump shots.

Why was the spider one of the most valuable members of the ball team?
It was good at catching flies.

What do catchers eat dinner from?
Home plate.

How does a trombone score a home run?
Slide.

ANDY: I can't play ball today. I caught a cold.
CAPTAIN: Congratulations. That's the first thing you've caught all year.

LOUIS: Hey, captain, where do you want me to
play?
CAPTAIN: How about at another school?

Knock-knock.
  Who's there?
Tire.
  Tire who?
Tire gym shoes—you're
about to trip.

Knock-knock.
  Who's there?
Randy.
  Randy who?
Randy marathon and
am I tired!

Knock-knock.
  Who's there?
Trampoline.
  Trampoline who?
Trampoline the grass is not allowed.

What would you get if you crossed a bowling alley
with a sewing class?
  Pins and needles.

What do you call a cattle tug of war?
  Beef jerky.

JESS: Do you jump rope much?

WES: No, just once each time the rope comes around.

BEN: Every time I throw a Frisbee, the dog jumps up, catches it, and runs off.

LEN: That sounds like fun.

BEN: It's getting pretty expensive, you know. It's not my dog.

How did Barbie, the dramatics teacher, help the chicken with its part in the school play?

Barbie cued the chicken.

Why didn't the teacher give the pig a part in the play?

He was a big ham.

Why did the thief want to be in the play?

So he could steal the show.

Why didn't the deer take anyone to the school dance?

It wanted to go stag.

Why didn't the chicken go to the school dance?
She was in a fowl mood.

Why didn't the owl go to the school dance?
It didn't give a hoot.

Why do some fish swim on the bottom of the sea?
Because that's where fish go when they drop out of school.

What kind of fish is good at Old Maid?
A card shark.

Why was the fish such a good musician?
He knew his scales.

Why did the music students get into trouble?
They were passing notes.

What do you call it when a violin player runs away?
Fiddler on the hoof.

What kind of music do old clothes like best?
Rag-time.

What kind of music did the door knocker like?
Rap.

What kind of music do insects like?
Bee-bop.

What kind of music do insects like to dance to?
Buggy woogie.

What musical instrument do cats play?
The mew-kulele.

What was the band's favorite lunch?
Tuba fish sandwiches.

14. TAKE ME TO THE NURSE

We had a test yesterday that was so tough, the school nurse had to be present before we could begin.

Why did the water snake need medical attention?
It felt eel.

What insect has trouble talking?
The hoarse fly.

What is the most cowardly disease?
Chicken pox.

What injections do rockets get?
Booster shots.

What pills do astronauts take?
Space capsules.

How did the sick frog get to the nurse?
He had to be toad.

Knock-knock.
  Who's there?
Amanda.
  Amanda who?
Amanda a great strain.

Knock-knock.
  Who's there?
Oslo.
  Oslo who?
Oslo and getting slower.

Knock-knock.
  Who's there?
Yule.
  Yule who?
Yule miss me when I'm gone.

What man in armor comes down the chimney on December 24?
The knight before Christmas.

What did one Christmas tree say to the other?
"I pine for you."

TEACHER: Our school nurse is in training.
LOUIS: Really? Whose is she going to fight?

NURSE: Stick out your tongue.
JUAN: What for? I'm not mad at you.

NURSE: I'd like to take your temperature.
DAVID: Why? Don't you have one of your own?

GLADYS: Nurse, nurse, I was just playing my
harmonica and I swallowed it!
NURSE: Lucky you weren't playing a piano!

JUDY: Nurse, nurse, I'm sick as a dog!
NURSE: I can't help you. I'm not a vet.

GWEN: My father's a doctor, so I can stay home and
be sick for nothing.
GLEN: My father's a preacher, so I can stay home
and be good for nothing.

15. SCHOOL'S OUT!

I'm glad they don't get Groundhog Day and the last day of school mixed up. I'd hate to see my shadow and have six more weeks of classes.

LUKE: During my vacation I'm going to do all the things I couldn't do during the school year.
DUKE: Like what—pass English?

Where are the birds going on vacation?
The Canary Islands.

Why is the mummy going on a vacation?
It needs to unwind.

TONY: I'm going to spend my vacation reviewing everything I learned at school.
JOAN: Really? What are you going to do the second day?

LAURIE: My teacher says that summer vacation is not the time to stop learning.
MAURIE: I agree. I stopped learning round about Christmas break.

Why is H the most popular letter of the alphabet?
It is the start of every holiday.

Knock-knock.
  Who's there?
Utah Nevada.
  Utah Nevada who?
Utah Nevada guess where we're going on vacation.

Why does the tire need a vacation?
It can't take the pressure.

Why don't sheep have enough money to go on vacation?
The rancher is always fleecing them.

Knock-knock.
  Who's there?
Midas.
  Midas who?
Midas well relax—no school all summer!

KIM: You remind me of a school that's closed for vacation.

TIM: How is that?

KIM: You have no class.

"What is one and one?"
  "Two."
  "What's four minus two?"
  "Two."
  "Who wrote Tom Sawyer?"
  "Twain."
  "Now say all the answers together."
  "Two two twain."
  "Have a nice twip!"

Knock-knock.
  Who's there?
Abyssinia.
  Abyssinia who?
Got to go—
Abyssinia!

INDEX